The Perils of Dating, Penelope!

STORIES FROM THE WORLD OF MODERN DATING

Kristen Houghton

& Sandra Morgan

Skylight-NYC Publishers
a division of Houghton & Hopper, LLC

The Perils of Dating, Penelope! Copyright © 2020 by Kristen Houghton

Part 1 Younger and (Somewhat) Naïve written by Kristen Houghton
Part 2 Older and (Somewhat) Wiser compiled by Sandra Morgan
Additional material in Part 2 written by Kristen Houghton

First edition

Library of Congress Cataloguing-in-Publication Data
Houghton, Kristen
The Perils of Dating Penelope, Houghton-1st. ed.
1. Non-fiction 2. women 3. dating
4. humor 5. True stories

Cover art by 2Hopper Production & Design Studio
Typesetting by KH Koehler Design

ISBN-13: 978-1-7324166-8-0

CONTENTS

Foreword

Simple question: Who is Penelope? Simple answer: Penelope can be the name for any woman who has ventured into the world of adult dating and has stories that are good and bad. Or she can be any woman who has stories, fiascos and triumphs, to relate to her friend Penelope. At some point we're either the friend who has the dating experiences or the gal pal we call up after a dating experience. In essence—we're all Penelopes.

Dating as an adult can be a somewhat perilous experience. I mean, come on, we're not teenagers simply thrilled to be going out with that "cute guy from English Lit" even though we know we are smarter than he is, have better manners, and are dreaming of a college-bound future to an Ivy League school whereas his aspirations are simply to get a job with the DPW in his local town. Nope, those days are—thankfully—behind us but as we go into our twenties, thirties, forties, and beyond, dating becomes more interesting and—alas more challenging.

Dating life has now gone from giggling teenage angst and the exciting but terrifying possibility of maybe "going all the way" to adult women contemplating whether a guy is worthy of being the one who will scratch her proverbial sexual itch. The mantra for going on an adult date today is similar to what Mel Brooks said in the movie *The Twelve Chairs,* "Hope for the best, expect the worst." Heaven help us, that's so true.

Dating someone new can be fraught with issues that we never even think of, let alone expect to happen. From having a very pregnant woman stalk you because you're dating *her boyfriend* and the father of her unborn baby, to going on what you thought was a romantic retreat only to find out the guy is into extreme bondage. From women who knowingly allow themselves to fall in love with the wrong man and suffer the heartbreak and pain when it ends, to women who are the target of scamming Lotharios and luckily realized it in time. The women in this book have many tales from the "dark side" to tell each other. See Penelope? Perils.

So to all the dating Penelopes out there, have a good read, a good laugh, and nod your head sagely if you see yourself and your dating experience in this book.

Just promise yourself one thing—don't give up on dating! You never know when a good guy will show up in your life.

~Kristen Houghton

Part One

Younger and (Somewhat) Naïve

The "Ex-tra" Needy Ex-Wife

We met at an art auction. Mark was handsome, funny, and about ten years older than I am. After drinks and a walk in Central Park, I found out to my delight that we had so much in common. I also found out that he was divorced from a woman named Ellen, had been divorced for over four years, and that they had two adult children.

"Our divorce was amicable and we're still on friendly terms. We actually still talk to each other about family things." How nice I thought. A guy who can still be friends with his ex. In hindsight, I should have asked just how "friendly" those terms were!

We dated for a month before becoming exclusive and I was happy. Our relationship was just beginning and I was all set to make it work. After all, I was certain that I could get along with his ex and his children. At that time, in the throes of a new hopeful relationship, I had no idea I would be competing with an exceptionally needy ex-wife.

Any relationship is meant to be between two people. Dealings with his friends, your friends, his parents as well as yours, are par for the course for any new couple—you can, and will, work that out. But throw a needy ex-wife into the mix and you're playing in a whole new ballgame, one for which you may not be prepared. If you're dating a man who is still tied to his ex, you may run into situations that can have a serious impact on your relationship. That is what happened to me.

The worst case scenario was that his ex-wife who, even after being divorced for over four years, still felt she could get in touch with her ex-husband—now supposedly committed to me—for every, and any, little problem in her life, day or night. I found out that he had a special ring tone on his phone just for her, something I wasn't sure I liked at all.

She didn't have a job—she had never worked outside the home when they were married and the kids were younger. Now she claimed intense anxiety and crippling migraines as her main cause for not seeking employment. Because of this, she lived solely on the generous spousal support from Mark.

I felt sorry for her—she was alone, after all—and I was trying to be the mature, sensible person about the situation. I mean, why worry? Mark was with me, right? He loved me. But as time went by I began to feel as if Mark was a little *too willing* to get up and run to her house every time she called or texted him.

The bonds of relationships are complicated and complex even when two people are no longer sharing a life together. It is aggravating to the ultimate degree to have your guy's ex-wife constantly calling him.

"Mark, I think someone broke into my car. Yes, I did call the police but can you please come over? I'm scared to be alone."

The police found no evidence of anyone trying to break into her car.

"Mark? I lost my keys and can't get into the house. I have no idea where the spare keys are. I looked and looked, but can't find them. You have the only other set of keys to the house. Is it too much trouble for you to come over here?"

Mark found the spare keys where she had always kept them—hanging from the keyring on a nail in the gardening shed.

"Oh, hello. Is Mark there? I need to speak with him. No, I don't want to leave a message. It's about a problem I'm having. What? Oh, no, thank you. You won't be able to help me. I'd rather speak with Mark about it."

The problem that time was that she couldn't open a bottle of wine and needed Mark's help. He went running over to help her, ended up having a couple of glasses of "their" favorite wine, and was gone for over five hours.

My new relationship with Mark was now being disrupted on an almost daily and nightly basis by a woman who was legally divorced from my man. She even used one of their children—a serious family matter, she said on the phone—to drag him over to her house.

I completely understand that when there are children in the picture, phone calls between the two ex-spouses are inevitable. Mark did have children with his ex but his daughter lived on campus at an out-of-state college and his son, who had already graduated from college, was working for an environmental organization and had an apartment in the city.

I had met both of his kids and we had gotten along very well. Mark's daughter actually confided to me that the reason she liked living on campus out-of-state was that her mother is "very manipulative and wants to be way too involved in my life." That sentence would stay in my mind and haunt my sleep. Manipulative. Too involved. Uh-huh.

The "serious" family matter Ellen called Mark about concerned their son. She called and told Mark that she was worried because "our boy" hadn't called her in a twenty-four-hour period.

"He calls me every day, Mark. I'm so upset. Please, can you locate him and tell him to call me? I am sick with

worry."

When Mark finally got hold of their son through his son's employer, the young man was annoyed. He said that his mother knew very well that he was going to be on an ecological retreat in a remote area and lack of phone service in that area meant he wouldn't be able to call her for three days.

Still, after he had called Ellen to assure her all was well with their son, Mark went running over to comfort her because this "trauma" had caused her to have one of her terrible migraines. When I suggested he call a doctor or the EMTs he replied, "What kind of man would I be if I couldn't comfort the mother of my children and get her through this pain?"

Uh, the kind of man who actually gets her medical help to deal with her migraines and anxiety? And by the way, what type of "comfort" are you offering Ellen, Mark?

Her neediness seemed to ratchet up when she found out that Mark had moved into my home. She began calling Mark to do things she could readily do herself or have done professionally. Picking up her car from the shop was no longer her ex-husband's concern, nor was mowing her lawn or re-grouting the tile in her bathroom, yet she always called him for these necessities. I told Mark that he had to make it clear to her that he would no longer be available for her "chores list." He nodded his head but, since the calls continued, I doubt he'd said anything to her at all.

Mark would get out of bed at 3:00 in the morning if she called. Hell, he'd even get out of bed during sex with me if his phone chimed with her ringtone. He would leave work to check on her if her anxiety was giving her a bad day. When she called, it seemed as if he jumped to go to her. And she called or texted way too often.

On what was supposed to be a romantic weekend in the Hamptons, he spent almost an entire night on the phone with her trying to calm her down because there was a thunder storm in her area and she was frightened. I was seriously beginning to think of calling for a cooling off period from Mark. I had just about had it with this needy ex-wife drama.

By sheer chance, the straw that would break this relationship's back occurred at a happy social event—his best friend's wedding reception. It was a pleasant affair and Mark and I were having a wonderful time. He was attentive, funny, and I began to think that maybe all would begin to go smoothly with our relationship.

Mark had gone over to the bar to get us drinks and left his phone on our table. The ringtone he had for Ellen began sounding. The first two times I let it go to voicemail. Then his phone buzzed with a text message. I picked up the phone and read it and my face flamed with anger. That was it. I was so done with his ex-wife's behavior. She texted Mark that she was "lonely," and her anxiety level was "really bad right now." Could he just stop by and check on her? And she obviously knew where we were because she asked him how the wedding ceremony had been.

When Mark came back with our drinks I showed him the message. "Can you believe this, Mark? She seriously needs to get professional help. This has to stop."

To my amazement, rather than be annoyed that she was doing this, he seemed to want to go to check on her.

"You can't be serious!" I hissed. "We're at a wedding reception. Dinner hasn't been served yet and you want to go check on her?"

"She's lonely, Jesse. She has anxiety problems and she needs me."

"What about me?" I asked quietly. "Don't you think I need you too?"

"You'll be fine. You're a strong person and, well, Ellen isn't. She needs me. I'm sorry, Jess. I have to go. I'll be back later."

I told him not to bother. That I'd call an Uber.

"Okay," he said, sounding relieved that he didn't have to come back and pick me up. "Thanks for saying that. Ellen's really stressed. I'll handle it. I'll see you back at your place."

I walked Mark outside to the parking area and as we waited for the valet to bring his car, I told him what I'd been thinking about. I told him not to come back to my place or to even call me again. I would have his things sent to Ellen's house since that seemed to be the place he really wanted to be.

"You made your choice, Mark. Go to her now and deal with whatever is happening in her life. It's clear you don't want to be in my life or our relationship."

"Jess, don't. I'll work it out. I really care about you. It's just that she has some problems. You understand, right?"

I shook my head and stood my ground. "No, Mark, I really *don't* understand and I don't care either. I want someone who is committed to our relationship, committed to me. I won't deal with this anymore. You made your choice. Your ex's problems are not my fault and I will not allow them to become *my* problems. It's over."

He glanced at his phone when it buzzed again. "I've got to go," he said. "I'm sorry."

Mark didn't *seem* all that sorry as he hurried to his car. I watched him drive away to his ex-wife and I felt a burden lift from my shoulders. Mark was right about one thing.

I am strong, too strong to allow someone's ex-wife to interfere with my happiness. The "ex-tra" needy ex-wife was *his* problem.

Stalked by My Boyfriend's Pregnant Girlfriend

t was an amazing meeting for me. My friends said that I was lucky to have found this guy. In retrospect, maybe unlucky would be a better word.

I met Glenn at an upscale bar, a place where a lot of us who worked in nearby offices would meet up on Friday nights for appys and drinks. He bought me a platter of shrimp eggrolls and we hit it off immediately. A couple weeks later, after we had met at restaurants, parks, and a museum for four dates, I felt comfortable enough to have him pick me up at my condo. I thought it was okay that he knew where I lived. Glenn told me that he was in the process of moving and his place was a mess of boxes and all, so I never found out his address. At the time, it seemed to be a trivial matter.

That's when it started getting very strange.

A week after our last date—a night when he had stayed overnight—I began to have the strange sensation that I was being followed. It's an uncomfortable feeling to say the least. I couldn't be absolutely sure, but I felt as if someone was following me from my condo to my office, and any place else I went.

Once in a grocery store I felt so uncomfortable about walking to my car that I asked store security to escort me there and wait until I was safely inside my car with the doors locked. The security man told me that maybe I should report being followed to the police.

"You might have a stalker on your case, miss."

I didn't call the police—I know I should have—but I didn't. However, I made sure to have pepper spray available and had an extra lock installed on my front door as well as safety locks on the windows even though my condo was on the third floor. You never know.

For some reason, I didn't immediately tell Glenn. Didn't want to worry him, didn't want him to be scared off if he thought there might be a dangerous element in this new budding relationship. All dumb excuses. I know. But when Glenn came to pick me for a movie date, he noticed the new locks.

"What's going on? I thought this was one of the safer neighborhoods," he joked half-heartedly.

"It is but, well, I think I might have a problem with someone stalking me."

I expected him to fear for my safety, show a look of deep concern, etc., hug me and ask if I was okay, but I received none of that. In fact, he didn't look surprised or even terribly concerned—he just tried to calm my fears by saying that maybe I was imagining it. I was probably overtired, overworked and, well, sometimes that creates irrational fear, he said. Glenn was nice and very sweet but my antenna went up at his lack of surprise and concern. I told him that I resented that he used the word "irrational" in reference to a possible real danger.

Something was definitely wrong. Our date that evening

was awkward with stilted conversation and a feeling of unease. When we went back to my condo, Glenn kept looking around almost as if he were looking for someone or something. Was he finally starting to show some concern for me?

But when we reached the steps of my condo, he begged off coming upstairs, saying that he had an early meeting the next morning and needed to sleep in his own bed. When I went in for a kiss, he looked around, backed away, then kissed my forehead. "Good-night. Sorry I'm just really tired. I'll try to call you tomorrow."

He obviously didn't try too hard. I never received a call.

A few days later, I glanced out the window of my condo and saw Glenn parked across the street from where I lived. In the passenger seat was another person, wearing an oversized hoodie. I opened the window, leaned forward, and waved to him. When he saw me leaning out the window he quickly drove off. I waited an hour and then called him. It went right to voice mail. The day turned into evening then turned to night and by Midnight, he hadn't returned my call.

A week went by with no contact from Glenn. I called and texted numerous times but he never responded. I didn't know where he lived so I couldn't go there to talk to him about his sudden lack of communication.

After another week of no response, I stopped trying to get in touch with him and chalked the whole time I spent with him up to a bad dating experience. I didn't know why—was he freaked out because I thought I was being stalked? Was he that insensitive to my fear? Or was the idea of dating someone who was being stalked a deal-breaker and too much to handle. I didn't know.

Meanwhile the feeling of being followed and observed continued.

Two weeks later, Glenn made another "appearance by car." He was back, parked in a different location near my building. As before, there was a second person in the car wearing a baggy hooded sweatshirt. I was starting to get freaked out. Who is that person? My gut instinct was kicking in and I felt a wave of fear.

But curiosity won and fear be damned. I went outside to confront him and ask why he was there and why he felt he needed a buddy for support. If he wanted to talk with me about why he'd been avoiding me, just talk. I didn't need this childish drama. When he saw me approaching he drove off— fast. What the hell was going on?

The next night, as I was entering my building, I saw his car pull into a space two buildings down. I hurried inside. This time I was through with all the bullshit—I was going to call the cops.

Before I hit 911, there was a knock on my door. I looked through the security opening in the door, expecting to see Glenn. I was so mad I didn't think straight. I was going to let this bozo have it. Who the hell did he think he was?

But it wasn't Glenn who was standing in front of my door. It was his buddy, the one in the oversized hoodie. I watched as the person pushed back the hoodie and I found myself staring into the eyes of a young woman.

A very *pregnant* young woman.

"Please open the door. I want to talk to you. I've been watching you. I need to talk to you about him, about Glenn. Please talk to me!"

She looked so sad and frightened that I opened the door and went into the hall. As soon as I was outside my door, she began to cry and asked me why I wanted to take her baby's father away. How could I date a guy with a pregnant girlfriend? Why was I doing this to her?

"I knew he would cheat on me again. I just knew it. I followed Glenn to your house. I had to see what you looked like. Glenn likes dark-haired women and you're his type. Once I knew where you lived, I came back and followed you to your office and everywhere you went."

"That's called stalking and it's a criminal offense. I can have you arrested," I said as calmly as I could, taking the warrior stance I'd been taught in a self-defense class. She might be pregnant but she was also filled with emotion and could become violent. I certainly didn't want to hurt her or her unborn child but I was more than willing to protect myself.

"I forced him to drive to your house at night and sit outside. I wanted him to confront you and break it off, but he wouldn't go up to your door. Stay away from my man, I mean it. He's all I have."

I let her go on for a while before I interrupted her and told her I had no idea he was in a relationship and about to become a father. "I don't date men who are involved with someone else. It's not me you should be angry with, it's him. Let's go to Glenn's car," I said locking my door. "I'll break it off right in front of you."

Surprisingly calm, I told Glenn what I thought about him and warned him to stay away from my condo, telling him I'd call the police in a heartbeat if I saw him on my street again.

"The same goes for you," I said turning to face his girlfriend. "The cops will not care if you're pregnant—as I told you, stalking is a crime. I will have you arrested and I will file charges. You understand?" Sobbing hysterically, she said she understood and got into the car.

My friends are amazed and shocked when I tell them about my very pregnant stalker. This was the strangest dating experience of my life and it has taught me a valuable lesson. I will always do a deep background check on anybody I may date. I want to know where they live. If they have nothing to hide, they won't mind letting me know.

No more "pregnant" surprises for me.

Married...But Not to Me

Being part of any couple can be challenging and unpredictable as we all know. But when the man with whom you're involved is part of *another* couple—meaning that he's someone else's husband—then the challenge and unpredictability can make your life a messy, unhappy waiting game which you will rarely win.

The woman who is in love with a married man, lives a life that, for the most part is shrouded in secrecy. Your close circle of friends might know about your affair but you really cannot let anyone else, such as colleagues or family, know. You are alone most of the time and spend it waiting—waiting for your married lover to call, to come meet you, to share some precious time together. You are not his wife, you are not mother to his children, you are not his parents' daughter-in-law. Your chance for happiness hinges on a future that is highly uncertain to say the least.

"I love him." This was always my heartfelt answer when my friends questioned me about being involved with a married man. "You can't help who you fall in love with."

My friends were never judgmental, just concerned about how I chose to live. "Alone" seemed to be my middle name. I was alone on weekends, alone on holidays, took vacations alone, attended weddings alone and canceled any and all plans I may have made for myself whenever Denis called.

And then there were too many times when, after I had canceled *my* plans with friends so I could be with him, that he called and said *he* couldn't make it after all. His excuse was always that he had "family obligations."

"Doesn't that bother you? That he calls and cancels?" asked a friend.

"Not at all, his family comes first, at least right now. I accept that."

And I truly believed that I did accept it at the present time.

I didn't tell my friends that Denis had told me that when his children were older he would file for divorce, that his marriage was only one of convenience for the children's sake—that I was his whole life and that he wanted me to wait for him to "be free."

I didn't tell them that I dreamed about marrying Denis and being a sophisticated, kind-hearted stepmother to his three daughters. I would have them over for holidays and weekends, take them shopping, never daring to try to replace their mother, just happy to be a loving older friend whom they would come to adore. Denis and I and his three girls would be a modern, happy step-family.

I had been with Denis for six years and the first three had been magical. We had met when he had come into the book store I owned to find an out-of-print children's book for his daughter's birthday. I *did* have the book in my shop but I was so impressed by Denis' good looks and his shy smile when he talked about his oldest daughter and her love of reading, that I lied and told him I had to order it and he could pick it up in a couple of days. I wanted to see him again.

And see him again I did. After buying the book, Denis asked me to have a late lunch with him as a thank you for having gotten him the book his daughter wanted so much. I accepted. It was to be the first of many lunches, dinners, and meetings for drinks we would share.

Denis also made it a habit at least twice a week to stop in my book store to just talk. He always brought coffee and hot scones for both of us which he got from an expensive gourmet shop nearby. While we drank the coffee, he would unburden himself about his unhappy marriage, his love for "my sweet little girls," and his sadness at how he was living a half-life with a woman who didn't love him. But he was kind about his wife, always saying what a great mom she was and how he was sorry that their marriage wasn't all he had hoped it would be.

I always listened intently and was very compassionate. This poor, unhappy man! Burdened with a loveless woman, only staying with his wife because he loved his girls so much and didn't want to leave them, trapped in a miserable life he hadn't ever expected. How courageous a man, how wonderful a father! With the smell of hazelnut crème coffee in the air and the gentle sound of his voice, I fell deeply in love with Denis.

The first time we made love I felt conflicting emotions. I was in love with Denis, yes, but this man who lay in my arms *was* married to another woman and a woman who was the mother of his children at that. How could I do this? I wrestled with the thought. I wasn't religious and I didn't feel that what I had done was a sin, still—there was the question of morality and what was right. Why was loving someone so totally complicated? It should be simple. Even while I was thinking these thoughts I knew I wanted to keep on seeing Denis and I knew that sex would always be a part of our being together. What we had done that afternoon had been tender and sweet. Should I feel guilt over sleeping with another woman's husband? I had never done anything like this before.

I felt *some* guilt about having a relationship with Denis,

but more than that, I felt a sense of uneasiness about who and what I was in Denis' life. Being with a married man, what exactly would my status be? I didn't want to be the proverbial "other woman." That term was not something I wanted to describe me. The old-fashioned term, mistress, was just ridiculous. And the word affair itself was too sordid a word for what I was getting into. I felt uneasy at what I was about to begin. What was I giving up to become someone who was merely a lady-in-waiting, a woman who would be living her life in the shadows, so to speak and who had no real claim on Denis in any way except in her bed?

Then I thought about how unhappy Denis was and how he had said that his unhappiness stemmed from a marriage to a woman who, mother of his children or not, didn't love him at all. The thought about his wife not loving Denis won my internal argument and I embarked on an affair with a married man letting any qualms about morality drift away. My love was a balm that would heal Denis.

The beginning of the affair was a heady and romantic period. Mostly we were content to stay in the book store or in my small house. I was in love and thrilled that Denis said he felt the same way.

There were date rules of course. One of them concerned Denis' fear of being found out. For example, when he came to my house he asked that the outside lights be turned off and the garage door open so he could drive his car into the garage without being seen.

We rarely went out, but when we did, we were careful to go places where we wouldn't be seen by any of Denis' friends or colleagues. Meeting at a restaurant, we never came together and I didn't enter until Denis had checked to see who was there and made sure we would have a table in an obscure area. It was sort of mysterious and exciting.

Holidays were bitter-sweet. He always tried to sneak away for a few hours but it was difficult. The rule here was that he would be the one to get in touch with me. *I* was never to try to reach *him*. It was the same when he went away on family vacations "for the girls' sake." No contact. I contented myself with brief phone calls or text messages.

During the first three years Denis talked about the future when his girls would be old enough to understand a divorce and to better handle the break-up of their parents. He intended to always be a strong and permanent presence in their lives and he couldn't wait for the day that I could also be a part of their lives as well. He mentioned how he and his wife really had "no relationship at all," the only thing they shared was parenting, and I believed he meant that there was no sexual relationship between them.

He earnestly told me that next to his daughters, I was the most important person in his life and how he hoped we could have a life together. When he talked like that, I basked in the daydreams.

Whenever my friends tried to fix me up with a "great unmarried guy," I thought of what I would eventually have with Denis and always said no thank you, adding, "You don't understand what we have together and what we *will* have in the future." My friends just rolled their eyes and sighed.

The fourth year of the affair brought changes. As his girls got older, it was getting harder and harder for Denis to get away. The twice weekly love-making sessions dropped down to one and then to once every two weeks. Going out was getting too risky—his oldest daughter was a teenager now and you never knew where you might run into her or one of her friends.

Commitments made were often broken and I would be disappointed over and over again, waiting and hoping. His children had sports, his oldest daughter was going through a problem, his wife needed him to drive the girls to a party. It seemed he talked incessantly about his children but now I wasn't as interested in them as before. I felt they were taking him away from her.

My friends still called with offers to set me up on dates with great single men they knew, but I stubbornly clung to the idea that Denis and I had a future together. I told my friends that everything was going well, but there were problems in our relationship that I didn't tell them.

One was that Denis no longer talked about divorce. If I mentioned our life together after he got his divorce he became vague and a bit angry. Seeing his reaction, I became afraid to mention it at all. Another problem was that he was doing more and more things with his family and those things included his wife. In fact, I was surprised and jealous when he canceled a long planned-for dinner with me because he had to visit a college over the weekend with his wife and daughter.

His simple statement—"I'm sorry I have to cancel but we've been talking about this college for our daughter for quite some time"—brought me to tears because this was something intimate he and *his wife* shared. He went on to tell me that their daughter was one of the few prospective freshmen staying as a guest in a college dorm. He and his wife would be at a hotel nearby.

While Denis said all this matter-of-factly, just the thought that he and his wife would be staying in a hotel room together for the weekend hurt me more than I ever thought it would. I was sure he wasn't going to sleep on a *couch* in that hotel room. The thought that he might have sex with his wife made me sick even while I realized that I had no right to feel that way.

The affair was continuing but there was a lack of excitement and passion in it now. Being alone ninety-five percent of the time was getting more difficult to take. Occasionally we still talked over coffee in the book store but I noticed that Denis was talking more and more about his life with his family. He no longer referred to his wife as the woman who was the cause of his unhappiness in a loveless marriage, now she was a person who, not only was a wonderful mother, but an intelligent woman who was going back to school to finish her Master's degree. He was proud of her. *She* needed his support and guidance. I couldn't help but feel jealous of this woman.

Yes, I was the "other woman," but hadn't I been the one who'd been there for Denis in his unhappiest moments? Hadn't I been the one who had comforted him with my love and my body? Did all my patience and sincere love mean nothing? Didn't he owe me more than to sit here talking with me about a woman who he had once said was ruining his life?

I had once seen a picture of his wife. I hated herself for doing it but one night while he was in the shower, I had checked his laptop. Going through his photo album I saw pictures of his daughters snorkeling on a family vacation. In one of the pictures there was Denis with his arm around a pretty blonde woman, laughing in the background. She looked contented and relaxed, the way a woman looks when life is going well. The picture's caption read "Mommy, Daddy, and the girls" I knew I wasn't meant to see that picture and quickly shut the laptop when I heard the shower stop.

Denis' visits became even more sporadic and I'd had nothing but text messages and emails, not even a phone call, for over a month when Denis finally did call and asked to meet me in the bookstore. I had a dread that I couldn't explain, a dread I'd had ever since he and his wife had gone together to look at a college for their daughter.

As soon as I saw his face I knew that this was to be our last time together. Denis had gotten to a place where he had had to make a hard choice about his life. He brought the usual coffee and scones and we went to sit in the back room of the book store. Before he'd even had a sip of his coffee, he came right to the point of his visit.

"Jenna, this is difficult for me. I love you very much, but I can't be with you anymore. I'm trying very hard to make my marriage work. My wife and I have been married for twenty-three years and I owe it to her to give it my best effort. She's been a terrific mother and loyal to me. I know we can make our marriage work now. Actually it's a new beginning for us, for me."

A new beginning? I was stunned. He owed the woman who had made his life miserable?! What about what he owed *me*? Did what we had mean so little to him?

"You will always be in my heart, Jen, but we just can't be together anymore. My family and my wife need me now. I know you understand. There's some wonderful man out there for you, a good single man with no ties. He'll be lucky to get you. I'm so sorry, honey. I have no choice but to do this."

I literally had nothing to say. Between us lay the unopened coffee containers and the unwrapped scones. He got up and kissed me. We both cried in each other's arms, and then, one quick kiss more and he was gone. As quickly as he had come into my life, he left. All those years of him being there and now he was gone to be with his family. *They* needed him. Now I was one hundred percent alone. I felt hurt, confused, and depressed.

I cried for over two weeks and I hate to admit it, but there were times when I thought about killing myself. He had hurt me so badly and the pain of his leaving me to return to his wife was terrible.

There comes a time when crying stops and reason takes over. The cold hard truth was that Denis had never had any intention of leaving his wife. I was only a diversion for him when he was going through unhappy times in his marriage. I had to face that fact.

When I was done crying, I made plans to go away for a long weekend near the ocean. I needed time to heal and begin to make positive plans for my life. Denis had his new beginning and I needed one as well.

On the beach watching the waves gently swirl to the shore and out again, I made a promise to myself. I would never, ever again allow myself to be the "other woman." I deserved a man who had no commitments. Denis was married, but not to me and that was a hard lesson to learn but, hard lessons have value.

I never forgot the value of that particularly hard, and bitter, lesson.

Falling in Love with My Gay Best Friend

He's good-looking, he's hot, smart, sophisticated, fun and sexy. Oh, and one more thing: He's gay. You *love* your gay male guy but would you risk falling *in love* with him? It's an issue that more than one woman has had to deal with in a relationship that is a perfect blending of everything except sex.

During the earliest days of my writing career my best friend Brett and I were in a situation that we liked to call "dateless dating," meaning that we weren't a couple but spent the so-called date nights with each other. Both of us involved in building our journalism careers, we had no time for significant others and so we did everything together—movies, Broadway, weekend candlelit dinners of pizza and wine. We even went on vacations together, and one time swam naked in the Gulf of Mexico at night. Everyone assumed we were in love but, truly, romance had no part in our relationship. We loved each other but we could never be *in love* and we never went beyond the quick greeting or parting kiss and hug. I respected Brett's sexual orientation as he respected mine. Our friendship was the most important issue for us.

Still, despite the no-sex part or possibly *because* of no sex, we had a great relationship. Walking through the park we'd hold hands, stay for sleepovers at each other's places after all night research sessions, and enjoy each other's company. We were so perfect "as a couple" that when we spent holidays together two years in a row, relatives began privately asking me "When's the big day?"

Though I fantasized about what it would be like to make love with him, in my heart I knew there wasn't going to be a big day for Brett and me—we were just great buddies! I loved him, he loved me, but as friends. Right?

Well, maybe.

Brett was always there for me and that was especially true one year after my life had some major upheavals. One Friday while we had our usual candlelight pizza and wine dinner, I poured my heart out to him. There were some unpleasant family and money issues going on, a deadline I had been damn-sure I'd be able to meet was looming with not much progress on my part, and my beautiful ancient car was giving me grief. Brett took me in his arms and we snuggled on the couch while I sobbed. He told me that I was just overtired and overwhelmed and that everything would be okay. He kissed my hair and held me close.

His arms were strong, he smelled so good, he was very male, and suddenly I was acutely aware that I wanted to have sex with Brett. Being in his arms was very arousing. I wanted him and I asked myself why not? I began to kiss him and, after a few minutes, he hesitantly kissed me back. I was the pursuer. I wanted him, I was in love with him, I needed him so badly. I removed my top and pulled my skirt up. Brett made a sound but whether one of protest or passion I couldn't tell. At that point I didn't care.

But, even in my over-tired and wine hazed mind two things made me consider what I was about to do and made me *not* do it. One was that I didn't want to embarrass Brett by making a move that would make him have to choose between doing something he didn't want to do or rejecting me outright. The second issue was our perfect friendship—a relationship I definitely prized and didn't want to ruin.

Eventually I fell asleep in his arms and woke up to find both of us had spent the night on the pull-out couch. Looking at him sleeping in all his innocence I decided that I had made the right decision. I wanted him in my life and would not risk losing what we had.

As time went on I had to acknowledge, even if just to myself, that I had had a major crush on Brett from the very beginning of our friendship. If he knew it, he never let on and I continued to enjoy our relationship the way it was even though I sometimes fantasized about us and looked to find more in his hugs than just friendship.

Eventually I met my love, my so-called soul-mate, and married him. To my great joy, my husband and Brett hit it off as friends, both of them inveterate Yankee fans.

Brett met his love too and a couple of years ago I was an attendant at their wedding. Before his big day I took Brett out for drinks. After his fourth Blue Moon, he told me something that was sweet and touched my heart.

"You know something Brooke? If things had been different, you know if *we* were different, I'd be marrying you tomorrow. That's how much you mean to me. You are a person I want to keep in my life. Do you understand what I'm saying?"

I nodded. Oh yes, more than you know.

Thank you, Brett.

I Don't Date Fat Girls

was going to a birthday party at the home of a friend from work who is a kind of matchmaker. There were going to be about twenty people meeting up at his house and I was looking forward to a fun evening. I was five-months-single from a relationship that had lasted a little longer than it should have because the guy was a starving artist-type and I cared enough about him to make sure he was on his feet financially before he moved out. Our break-up was an amicable and no-hard-feelings break-up and I was feeling good about starting a new chapter in my life.

My co-worker David is a kind man in a happy relationship and he likes playing Cupid for his friends. At the law firm where we work, colleagues tease him because he wants everyone to be as contented as he obviously is. So when he told me he had the "perfect guy" for me, a buddy he'd worked with at another firm, I played along and thought what the hell? It might be fun.

David's wife greeted me at the door with a glass of Sangria and showed me where the birthday boy was sitting talking to a good-looking guy about his own age. His wife whispered to me that David was singing my praises to his friend Rob and she couldn't wait to see what would happen.

"Who knows, Lindsay?" she said. "You and Rob might be a perfect match." I laughed and decided to watch David in action. David spotted me and winked then pointed to where I was standing.

"That, my man," I heard David say a bit loudly, "is the woman I was telling you about. Lindsay is fantastic! She's traveled around the world twice, knows her way around Rome as easily as she does New York City *and* she's just made partner at our law firm. You should meet her. You two might have a lot in common. She's—"

"*Fat*. I don't date fat *girls*," Rob said abruptly not even bothering to lower his voice.

His statement made an immediate impact on those in the room. Everyone was silent, discreetly sneaking peeks at me, the "fat" woman standing near the French doors that led to the garden. His words stung and I had a hard time moving. I felt as if I was frozen in place. Frozen in place with white-hot anger, if such a thing is possible. I was pissed.

Several women standing near him told Rob point blank that he was an idiot and really, who was *he* to judge someone? David agreed with the women. A couple of men shook their heads at Rob's totally unacceptable comment. I just stood there holding my glass of Sangria and simply stared at this incredibly rude man.

I am one of those people who have had to fight weight all their lives. To be completely honest, I have never weighed what the charts say I should. I'm not the correct number on the scale according to my gynecologist, who is so thin he looks like an eel with feet, but I'm hardly a candidate for that show *My Six-Hundred Pound Life* either. I carry about thirty curvy extra pounds on my five-five frame.

Even though I'd just attended my twenty-fifth college reunion, what Rob said about not dating fat girls sent me back to my dateless college days.

Dating back in college was a horror for an overweight girl. College men chose skinny girls over the fuller-figured ones any day and getting a date for an event became a nightmare. Never mind that I had a 4.0 and was on the Dean's List, never mind that I was the editor of my college newspaper or that I was a published poet, never mind that people praised my taste in clothes or that I always had a smile on my face. Forget that I made sure I was always up-to-date on world news so that I could converse on just about any topic. None of that mattered on date night.

The same young men who asked for my help in Composition and Rhetoric or Advanced Statistics, didn't know I existed when they were looking for a date for Friday night. They gave me a casual "Hi" as they passed me by on campus or in town on a week-end evening. They were looking for a hot date and I didn't qualify.

To make matters worse, my female friends were all thin girls who bordered on anorexia in their attempts to be thin and popular. One girl in my dorm had allergies to many different foods. She had very little choice in what she could eat and that kept her thin and gorgeous. This poor girl literally *couldn't* eat and I envied *her*!

It seems ridiculous to me now that I also envied one particular friend who could binge and purge at will. But sticking my finger down my throat after eating was something that I just couldn't do. I *thought* about it, believe me, I really did, but I just couldn't *do* it.

I even envied my reed thin, always sick, constantly constipated cousin, who had no problem getting a date whenever she chose. I, who had superb health, was jealous of these people because boys wanted to be with *them*. I was a fun person—why didn't anyone want to get to know the real me? What was so terribly wrong with me?

What was wrong with me was I didn't fit the image of what a college girl should look like. The extra weight was a stumbling block to popularity and dates, and eventually to my self-esteem. It had a domino effect on my life.

The more upset I became about my body, the less care I took of my appearance. I pulled my hair back into a severe ponytail and wore no makeup. The pretty clothes, larger sized though they were, were left in the closet and I took to wearing sweats and any baggy top I could find. No one was going to ask me out anyway I reasoned, why even try? The more I despised my body, the more I punished it by eating. It was a no-win situation.

I punished my body through my twenties in law school and into my thirties. Then a miracle appeared in the form of a judge where I was assigned to clerk. She was not stick-thin as society and fashion dictated. She didn't appear to be unhappy with her body and dressed magnificently, accenting her curves, and wearing colors I had always been told would not look good on anyone who wasn't "slender." On her they looked great.

Judge Hamilton was an active woman who loved dancing and playing tennis and had a tremendous amount of confidence. That impressed me as much as her popularity with others who worked in the courthouse. I was in awe of her and admired her tremendously. Being in her presence, hearing her talk about her life, her husband, the fun things they did, was like therapy for me. She inspired me to be positive about life and to have fun.

Tired of feeling down about my body image, I began to emulate her. With effort and determination, I began playing tennis, albeit in sloppy sweats. Sitting alone in my condo became something I did only when I wanted absolute quiet to study or work on briefs. I began shopping for a new wardrobe and had highlights added to my shoulder-length auburn hair. I began to like and appreciate myself more and more.

At the breakfast the day before my clerkship was finished, I went up to Judge Hamilton and told her what an impact she had made on my life, the way I thought about myself, and my weight.

She looked at me and, with a smile, asked if I felt healthy and happy. When I said yes, she said that was all that mattered and that she was glad she had made a difference in my life. She also said:

"Just remember that weight is subjective. One person's idea of overweight is another's person's idea of just right. No one should tell you what is good for you. That's your decision. I've always been happy with my body and never wanted to weigh a number that I have to constantly struggle to maintain. Life is for enjoying. I'm happy with me and I hope you are happy with yourself, too. No one should set rules for how you should feel."

She was right and I never forgot that bit of advice. That's one of the reasons I won't starve myself. I like where I am and I like me. I'm not ashamed of my body.

I determined that I would control the evening and not some jerk who "doesn't date fat girls." I walked around the room stopping to talk to several groups of people. I was charming as I told hilarious stories of my travels, my law school classes, and modestly accepted congratulations on having made partner. Soon I had people seeking me out, asking about my travels, and telling silly lawyer jokes. Several people asked me to sit with them at the tables that had been set up on the patio. I chose the one with David and his wife and deliberately sat next to Rob, the "fat-hater." Then I began conversations with everyone at the table except him. Rob couldn't help but notice that the other men in our area were all interested in talking to me. Was he actually getting jealous because I was ignoring him?!

When dinner was finished and, as the night wore on, people got up from their tables and began milling around, getting drinks from the bartender and chatting in groups. I told David that I was going to get a Negroni and began walking over to the bar.

"Lindsay?'

I turned and looked at the person who called my name. It was Rob. He had been quiet and aloof when I first joined David's table on the patio but I'd seen him watch me interact with the other men.

He smiled and asked what I was drinking. "Something like red wine to match that sexy dress you're wearing? I'll get your drink." He was actually flirting with me!

"Thank you, no. I'll get it myself."

If I'm not Rob's type, that's his problem. If he can't see beyond what his *imagined* perfect woman is, then he will miss out on a being with a lot of interesting, successful women. To tell the truth, Rob was rather boring. At the table he had no opinion on politics, Broadway plays, or books. He didn't care to travel and he basically had nothing much to say.

It was getting late and as I went over to say goodnight to my hosts, Rob approached me once more. "If you need a ride, I'll take you. I heard you say you came here by Uber."

At that moment, another guest, an attractive man I knew from my office, walked over to say goodbye to David. He looked at me and asked if I'd like to have a nightcap at a new rooftop bar nearby. He'd be happy to drive me home later

"Yes, I would. That would be lovely."

"Um," said Rob petulantly, "I believe *I* asked you first. I'll drive you home. Besides, David practically set us up. You kind of owe me this. Like a first date, you know?"

I looked right at him. "You're—Rob—right?" I deliberately pretended that I didn't remember his name. He nodded, annoyed.

"Well, Rob, I'm sorry, but you see, there isn't going to be any first date for you and me."

"What? You're seriously saying no to me? What's the problem?"

"Oh, no problem on my part. It's just that—*I* don't date shallow *boys*," I said.

I left with the guy who asked me to go for a nightcap. Rob just stood there embarrassed and bewildered.

Weight *is* subjective and we will never meet everyone's criteria of attractive. There is no reason to try to reach a pre-set goal created by society's "one-size-fits-all" mentality. Be yourself. Let the "Robs" of the world take note. I'm not here so *you* can approve of me and like me—I'm here to approve of, and like, myself.

I've learned that I'm very good at both.

Swipe Right for Mr. Wright

I never thought that I would use a dating app to help me meet "that certain someone." But two years after my divorce, I was looking to find, if not the love of my life, at least a man with whom I could share some fun things in life. I had tried joining groups of people who were interested in art, sports, and cooking. Nothing there. It was very disheartening.

I needed something a little more person-to-person focused yet I was wary of dating sites. My friend at work, Denise knew about my desire to meet someone. She'd met her fiancé through a dating app.

"Why not try one?" she asked me. "You never know if that special someone is out there just waiting for you. Your live-in mate."

Laughing at her sweet enthusiasm, I told her my intention in meeting someone was not for marriage. I just wanted to maybe date. Have some fun. Enjoy life with another person. Maybe get to know someone well enough so that—well, you know.

"The proverbial sexual itch, right. Got it. Uh-huh, got it. So—you mean a hook-up. That's different. For that you want Tinder.com. Needless to say, no one is on Tinder with the intentions of meeting the love of their life but, maybe you'll meet someone who's fun to be with, you know what I mean."

I must have looked apprehensive as hell because she tried to allay my fears and sound positive as she said, "Don't worry. It's really easy, Ella."

Okay, I thought, I could probably do this. Why not? According to my friend, *a lot* of people she knew went through this app. All I had to do was put up a nice pic of me, write a brief personal profile—the briefer the better I was advised by Denise—and I would be ready to begin my "romantic search." That sexual itch was getting pretty strong.

Denise walked me through the process. "You scroll through pictures and profiles of the guys there and when you find one that you might be interested in knowing, you swipe right. You can look at as many pics as you want and then make a choice. Really simple."

Sounded easy enough.

So with some trepidation, I set up my profile, found a picture where I looked pretty and relaxed and began my journey. Tinder requires people to log in using their Facebook profiles, because, you know, you can trust Facebook bios—no one lies on Facebook, right?

Yeah, right.

But I followed instructions and pretty soon I was set up on Tinder and ready to give it a whirl.

Now on this app, like so many others, it's all based on looks. You have a choice to swipe left if you're not interested, or right if someone catches your eye. Your choices are solely based on looks and a small biography. Kind of the adult version of being at a high school dance and being judged on whether you fit the adolescent boys' concept of the word "pretty." In other words, boys would rate you on the following—is the girl wearing glasses, braces, or is she what a teenage boy considers "ugly."

In the case of Tinder, it was pretty much the same type of scrutiny, albeit from the safety of the computer screen and not from the huddle of a bunch of teenage friends. Age doesn't change those attitudes. It seems that men haven't evolved all that far from the hormone-raging boys they once were, sad to say. I'm thirty-eight and attractive but it seems the average thirty-eight-year-old man wanted a "twenty-something, pretty, hot, sexy-looking woman." Good Lord! High school all over again!

I gamely checked the pics and profiles, not really finding someone I'd want to hook-up with or even have a cup of coffee with. And to top it off, no one seemed interested in getting to know me either. Discouraging for sure. Truthfully, I was getting annoyed. Is this all there is for the dating scene? Isn't there a better way to meet someone? Damn!

Then, one night unable to sleep and watching a forgettable movie at 2:30 AM, I heard my phone ding a message. Surprise, surprise—someone had swiped right for me.

His name was Jason. His picture showed a man who looked between thirty and forty—his profile said thirty-six—who had a nice smile, the kind of smile where a person's eyes crinkle up with happiness. His brief profile stated that he liked the beach and was a passionate lover of Broadway musicals. Nothing more, but I was intrigued by that smile.

I waited a day before I decided to send Jason a message. I was upfront. Why not be honest I thought. I said that I thought he was cute and that I was a total nutcase for the beach and Broadway. That alone made it seem as if we'd have a good thing in common.

He agreed and texted me later that day. Now usually Tinder meet-ups, well, actually *meet up* within a short period of time. But that didn't happen with Jason and me. I was anxious to meet him but almost relieved when it didn't happen right away.

For two weeks we messaged back and forth getting to

know each other a little more, a rarity on sites like Tinder. When the question arose of why we had both chosen Tinder and not an app more conducive to dating and not just hooking up for sex, it turned on a light about the realities of dating in the twenty-first century. Both Jason and I were divorced and what my friend Denise called the proverbial sexual itch was a high priority for us. Neither one of us had ever been promiscuous and we were kind of unsure why we would choose an app that seemed to be made simply for that. However, we both made it clear that sex would be part of our relationship when we did meet.

We were cautious. It turned out that we both lived in Florida on the Gulf Coast, about thirty minutes apart, and both of us were New York City transplants. After the two weeks were up, I boldly asked him to meet me for dinner at a restaurant in an area we were both familiar with, a casual place near the beach. If sex was a topic that would be on the table—no pun intended—so be it.

When we finally met in person, it was a little like reconnecting with an old friend. He was very nice-looking, tall, and slimmer than the head shot of his profile pic had shown. I felt a bit uneasy as I watched him carefully check me out when he thought I wasn't looking. But when he smiled at me I knew that the evening was going to be a good one even if a relationship wasn't formed and being together didn't go past this one night. I was okay with that. We talked about the sexual part of getting together and finally agreed that more than one date was needed for *that* to begin.

A month went by and we saw each other five more times. Even though we both were shying away from sex at this point, I could tell by his erections whenever we kissed that, physically, he desired me.

The following month, Jason was gone on an extended business trip but called me almost every night. And it was during that time, that I noticed that Jason had taken down his profile from Tinder. I did the same.

When Jason came home we had sex for the first time and I had my proverbial sexual itch more than satisfied. It was a fantastic experience for both of us and we're both glad that we got to know the intellectual person before we got to the physical.

We've been together for three and a half years but neither one of us wants to get married right now. It's good the way we are. Maybe someday, but for now, this is what we both want.

Jason and I have a little joke that we tell people who ask how we met.

"Well, you know how you can swipe right if you're interested in a person?" I say.

"She did just that," laughs Jason. "She swiped *right* for Mr. Jason *Wright*!"

Part Two

Older and (Somewhat) Wiser

Surprise! Bondage

When you're over fifty, newly divorced, and finally entertaining the idea of entering the dating scene for the first time in almost thirty years, it can be a little frightening—and exciting—all at the same time. So, when I decided to jump in, I then had to figure out how I was going to meet someone, never thinking for one minute that it would be so hard. After all, I worked in the corporate world and was surrounded by men every day. This should be a piece of cake, right?

However, I quickly found out why the adage "don't dip your pen in the company ink" has merit and should be paid attention to and strictly forbidden. I only dated two guys from my office and both dates turned out badly to say the least.

I then turned to my friends and asked if they knew any nice, single men that might want to date me. One friend who shall remain nameless because she's still hiding from me, introduced me to a very nice, good looking man whom she had known for over ten years.

"You two are a match made in heaven," she said. "He's also divorced and has grown children." That statement was a big plus since one of my recent dates had a three-year-old from his second marriage to a much younger woman. "He's just gotten back in the dating scene, too. This is going to be great!"

She arranged for us to meet at a local coffee shop that weekend. Entering the coffee shop, I was immediately greeted by a very handsome, well-dressed man with salt and pepper hair and a neatly trimmed beard. He stated that he instantly recognized me from the description my friend had given him. I was taken aback a little, but he was so sweet as he lifted my hands, introduced himself and placed a soft kiss on top of my right hand.

"Did you recognize me?" he asked looking up at me.

"Not at first since she didn't tell me you had a beard, but, now that I see those steel blue eyes, I knew it had to be you because they are just as she described them."

He walked me over to a table he was saving and as we sat down, he said he just knew this was going to be a great first date. From that moment, it seemed like we were on the path to discovering something magical.

We met for dinner almost every night for the next two weeks and spent the weekend going to antique shops and a few local farmers' markets. He was the perfect gentleman, always opening doors, pulling out chairs, and making sure I was happy. Secretly, I kept hoping he would make a move because I hadn't been so physically attracted to anyone in a long time. However, all that ever transpired was a gently placed kiss on my lips at the end of our dates which left me wanting so much more.

On our tenth outing, we were enjoying a lovely meal outside on a secluded patio of what had become our favorite restaurant when he leaned over to ask a question.

"Will you consider coming away with me this weekend?"

I think my heart literally skipped a beat or two from sheer anticipation as I fought a strong urge to leap across the table and jump him right there. I quickly reminded myself that I needed to at least try to play hard to get. But, I blurted out a very audible *yes* without asking any details.

He said he would pick me up on Saturday and that we were heading up to wine country to a beautiful little hotel tucked away in the mountains. My head was spinning as I began to fantasize about what our time together would be like. I told him I couldn't wait, and he stated the same as he gently kissed the palms of my hands, got in his car and drove away.

I had to wait two excruciatingly long days before the weekend finally came and as I packed, I began to get nervous. What should I wear? I should have prepared better, bought a negligee or something sexy. But what if he isn't planning to have sex? What if he is and changes his mind when he sees me naked? After all, my body doesn't look like it did when I was twenty. Hell, it doesn't even look like it did when I was forty! What if I'm terrible in bed? I haven't had sex since I was married, and let's face it, in the last few years of marriage, having sex with my ex wasn't high on my priority list. What the hell was I thinking when I got back into this whole dating thing? That no one would ever want to have sex with me again, basically that's what I was thinking.

And now, here I am.

I reassured myself that he knew I was over fifty and that we'd discussed the fact that I didn't believe in plastic surgery. He would just have to be okay with the fact that I didn't have a twenty-year-old body anymore. He always said that it didn't matter to him, and that he thought I was beautiful. So, I tossed out that ugly self-talk and closed the overnight bag.

He picked me up in his Jeep, and the drive up to the villa was splendid. We talked and laughed the whole way. I kept thinking that this must somehow be a dream because never in my wildest imagination could I have predicted this whirlwind romance.

Once we arrived at the villa, he escorted me inside and

asked if I wanted a glass of wine. As he brought me the glass, he asked if I minded him taking a quick shower and freshening up a little.

"Of course, I don't mind," I said shyly.

He said he'd hurry as he walked toward the bedroom. I noticed that he didn't grab his overnight bag. Now my mind was really racing. Was he making his move? Was he contemplating having sex right now? What should I be doing? Should *I* take a shower first? Why didn't he take his bag? Is he putting his clothes back on? Is he going to be naked? I just stood there in the middle of the living room watching him leave with a big goofy smile on my face.

He closed the door and I heard the shower running. After a few minutes he turned it off. I was still standing in the middle of the room staring at the bedroom door when called me and said. "Come here."

I reached down into my blouse, pulled my ever-elusive boobs up into my new French bra, tousled my hair, and opened the door. Here we go!

I was in for the totally unexpected.

There, standing next to the bed was this man I had been dating, wearing nothing but black latex underwear, holding handcuffs in his left hand and a whip in his right hand. On the bed next to him were all manner of bondage sex toys, leather masks, ball gags and latex outfits that I am guessing were meant for me.

I have no idea what the look on my face told him as I closed the door, grabbed my things and ran out of the room. I don't know if it was a look of shock or disbelief or one of sheer WTF on his face and I didn't care. I headed straight to the front desk where they ordered a cab that took me to the nearest car rental place.

My hands were shaking so badly I couldn't grip my wallet to take it out of my purse to pay the cab driver. As I entered the car rental building, my mind kept racing with a hundred jumbled questions. Was I so out of touch with the dating scene that I missed signs that he was into this kind of thing? Do men actually think you'll be into that stuff without asking first? And lastly—I had to laugh at this question—would I have *even fit* into those latex outfits?

As far as dating goes, I have to think that you just never know who you're going to meet. After a few weeks I went back into the dating scene as a more cautious and careful woman. I won't be fooled again by manners and fine dining.

This woman is on the lookout for any *Fifty Shades of Grey* warning signs.

The Scam Artist and the Older Woman

As a single woman, you eat alone—a lot of the time. Don't get me wrong, I'm completely okay with living alone and for the most part, eating alone. But there are times when I just want to be around people. So, I go sit at my favorite local bar where I feel safe and have been a Thursday night patron for over five years, and imbibe in a nice glass of cabernet sauvignon, savor a delicious meal, and engage in a little chit chat and laughter with my fellow regular bar mates. The night I met this charming scam artist was one of those nights.

A group of us had all arrived at our designated barstools around the same time, and had begun a lively conversation about our workday, our kids, grandkids, and so on. A good-looking, well-dressed gentleman in his sixties walked through the door, sauntered up to the seat next to me, said hello, asked if anyone was sitting there, and when I said no, sat down. He ordered a double scotch neat and leaned forward to survey the crowd gathered around the bar. He seemed extremely satisfied with what he saw and settled back into his seat.

One of my guy friends sitting on the other side of me struck up a conversation. "Haven't seen you here before. You from around here?"

"No," the handsome stranger said, "I'm from Austin and just passing through town."

"Well, welcome to our favorite bar," we all said in what seemed like a rehearsed pitch for the restaurant straight from a script for that popular 1980's show *Cheers.*

He had a very gregarious personality and was soon in the thick of everyone's conversations, especially mine for some reason—laughing and leaning into me like he'd been part of my life and the group for years.

Suddenly, and very loudly, he asked a peculiar question that set the tone for his next statement. "My name is Tom Green. Let me ask everyone a question: Do you prefer local bars like this, or more of a chain type bar to hang out?"

We all answered in a chorus, "We *love* our local bar, and we hate chains!"

"Great, I'm a journalist for a magazine and I would like to interview all of you for a story I'm writing on small local bars and their attraction."

This proclamation changed the whole mood of the establishment from one of friendly caution to friendly comradery. Drinks and food were on the house for this guy and he was center stage reveling in his newfound notoriety.

I must admit, that I was drawn into his ability to dazzle.

He whipped out a notepad and pen from his jacket and began interviewing a few individuals as well as groups of people in the bar. He wrote down their names making sure to spell them correctly, where they were from and then took a few pictures of the bar and its inhabitants. People also took photos with him on their phones, including me and a few of my bar pals. There was a lot of laughter and drinks flowing throughout the place as people thronged to get the chance to speak to him. He willingly obliged and as the interviews slowed down, he walked back to his seat, sat down and turned his attention towards me. I was flattered as he said, "Finally, I get to talk to the prettiest lady in the whole place."

We sat talking for hours, it seemed. It's amazing how a few drinks will loosen lips as I sat, telling this man I barely knew, my life story: Twice divorced, kids, successful business owner, tired of dating—the usual. Finally, I was ready to head home.

He quickly said, "I'm only in town for a few days, can I call you tomorrow? I'm staying at a hotel right down the street. I sure could use a friendly face to talk to and maybe take to dinner while I'm here for the next few days interviewing people."

My answer was sure, why not? He appeared to be a very trustworthy guy, after all he was a journalist for a magazine. It might be fun!

My friend, Jerry who was a local policeman stopped me on my way out and said, "Do you trust this guy?"

I shrugged. "He seems harmless. Why would someone lie about being a journalist for such a popular magazine?"

"Yeah, maybe you're right." Jerry said while giving this guy the once over.

Tom called the next day and we made plans to meet for dinner that evening. We agreed to meet there around seven. My workday was crazy, so when his text came in, I got all giddy and just as quickly became a little suspicious. He stated that he had never been more excited to see someone, and he just knew we were going to hit it off! He saw a real romance blooming in our future. My stomach did a little flip—but not in a good way—when he included the words *big kisses, two red hearts and a hug emoji* in his message. I didn't send a text in response.

I've learned in my years on this earth to listen to my instincts—they never prove me wrong. Who sends messages like that to someone you just met the night before?

The internet is a glorious tool. You can find almost anything online if you know how to search the topic. Luckily for me, online research was part of my daily business tasks and I had become very good at it. I went to the magazine website and did some digging into their contributors, but I couldn't find his name anywhere. That didn't raise any red flags because they didn't publish a list of their writers. So, I went to LinkedIn and did a search on his name, location and the name of the magazine. Nothing. Then I called the magazine. Again, nothing.

Red flags were starting to pop up, so I called Jerry, told him the whole story, and had him do a little research. I had taken a group photo that night at the bar and sent him the picture stating it was the guy sitting to my left. He said it wasn't a whole lot to go on, but he would see what he could find. My phone rang a few hours later and I was told this guy had a long list of aliases that immediately popped up when he scanned in the photo. His next statement ran chills down my spine.

"You need to stay away from this man, far away. He has conned over fifty unsuspecting people, mostly older women throughout the United States, out of hundreds of thousands of dollars. Can you tell me where you're meeting him? He has a long list of warrants out for his arrest. I plan to meet him there."

He never showed up at the restaurant. Maybe my lack of response threw up some red flags for him, but he fled in a hurry. I'll never know what tipped him off or what really happened. When they located the hotel he was staying at, and searched his room, they found clothes hanging in the closet along with a box full of fake ID's, fake hair pieces, beards and mustaches. He also left the list of names he'd written down from the bar with notations by each name on how he could take advantage of every individual he met that night. My friend, Jerry said he was probably long gone. Most of these grifters don't stay in one place more than a few days. They move on from town to town, create a new identity and take advantage of unsuspecting, vulnerable people.

It's been a little over a year since this happened so the sting of it all has faded. Now, when a stranger comes in for a drink at the bar, the first question and running joke is, "Are you a journalist?"

"Always, always trust your gut instinct. If you feel something's wrong, it is..." Kristen Houghton, *For I Have Sinned*

How Old Are You? Understated and Under-Aged

I n the world of online dating it's common to meet someone that lives in your own city, out of state, or even out of the country. You strike up a "conversation" and sometimes take it even further to a "real" conversation via a phone call or meeting in person at a local Starbucks for coffee.

Having met and gone out with several men I had connected with on dating sites open to all ages, I had grown tired of being hit on by men ten-to-twenty years younger than me. Although it was flattering, all I was searching for was someone my age or older that I could have an intelligent conversation with, who knew Paul McCartney when he was "with" the Beatles and didn't have an ex-wife—or several—with four children under the age of five.

So, I tried a popular dating site for the over fifty generation where I assumed—and oh, yes, I know the silly connotation behind the word assume—I would meet men my age, or older. That's where I met Ren.

Ren lived in the same city, was very witty on his profile, intelligent and yes, very handsome with salt and pepper hair, over six-feet in height, and rugged features. The height is definite requirement for a woman over five-foot-ten who has a closet full of high heels.

We struck up a great conversation hitting on the usual topics.

"Are you really over six feet tall?"

"Oh yes, I'm six-four."

Tall is good. I was salivating already.

"Have you ever been married?"

"No, and I've only been in one serious relationship."

Maybe a red flag, but at least there weren't any ex-wives.

"Do you have any children?"

"No, and not really looking to have any."

Again, might be a red flag but at his age—profile stated sixty-three—maybe he's not thinking with genitalia and doesn't want to be eighty when his kids graduate from high school.

"Are you a homebody?"

"Not all the time, I like to go out too and have fun."

Good answer.

This went on for a few weeks and we began having amazing online chats that lasted for hours. At this point, I really wanted to meet this man in person. He lived in my city and I felt like we had a lot in common so, when he asked if I wanted to meet for coffee I said, yes. I sent him my phone number in case he needed to cancel. He sent me his in turn stating that there was no way he was cancelling.

The day of our date was a Saturday and we agreed to meet at a local coffee shop and that it would be casual attire. I picked out a cute outfit that didn't shout, *she's trying too hard to look young*, but also didn't make me look like my eighty-year-old mother. Hopes in place, I set off to meet this dashing six-foot four-inch man with salt and pepper hair named Ren.

I was fifteen minutes early because I wanted to find a spot where I could see the front door and he could easily find me. Going on a Saturday was probably a bad idea because the crowd of people going in and out was crazy and I couldn't get a clear shot of everyone entering the coffee shop.

As I sat watching the door for the face from his profile that I'd fantasized over for almost two weeks, this young man with blond hair wearing skinny jeans that hung below his red boxers, and a ratty looking t-shirt with a backpack slung over his shoulder walked up to my table and smiled at me.

"Laura?"

"Yes?" I responded.

"I recognized you right away."

"You have me at a loss because I don't recognize you."

"Oh, yeah, like ummm, I'm Ren."

I must have stared at him for a full five minutes before responding with, "You're who?!"

He chuckled, pulled out a chair, answered a text message, laid his cellphone on the table and said, "I know what you're thinking."

I don't think he even had facial hair yet, and probably had only a few pubic hairs, and here he was sitting at a table with me grinning from ear-to-ear like he'd just pulled off the biggest hoax.

The answers to my questions I had asked him early on in our texting started raging through my addled brain. Oh my God, I finally thought, this guy is barely over five feet tall and the only long-term relationship he'd had was probably with his mother!

"No, I don't think you know what I'm thinking," I finally answered him. "Just how young *are* you?"

"I'm legal, if that's what you're asking."

"Wait, seriously, what the hell is going on? Is this a prank? Did one of my friends put you up to this?"

Again, he chuckled, picked up his cellphone, answered another text message and said, "Look, if you knew how old I was, you wouldn't have talked to me and I really like older women."

Immediately I thought, who does that? Sure, I know women who date younger guys and that it's socially acceptable now so—why lie about it on a dating site? At that moment, my curiosity turned to anger, and then back to curiosity again.

"Listen, just answer one question, all right? Just how young are we talking about here? Young enough to boost my ego or young enough to get me arrested?"

"I just turned nineteen last Thursday."

"Nineteen?!" The coffee I had just taken a large sip of came flying out of my mouth and spewed all over his cellphone.

"Whose photo did you use in your profile?" I finally asked.

"Oh, that's my dad."

I grabbed my purse, stood up, and with the best mom face I could make, I said—

"Your dad, huh? Is he single?"

Fed and Fucked—Seriously?

"Wise men talk because they have something to say. Fools talk because they have to say something." Plato

As an older, single woman, in the twenty-first century, I have come to the realization that the dating world has become significantly more complex than it was in my twenties. Looks, height, and body type are no longer the only significant parts of the initial attraction. If these characteristics are a game changer, then you are in trouble. Gravity has taken its toll. Personality, values, and honesty become paramount in the eyes of women who have loved and lost or never loved at all. The field of choices is limited and with age comes baggage—mine and his.

Life is messy and if you reach the midpoint of life and

beyond, there is going to be baggage. Dating after my life as a wife has been fraught with challenges, some good, and some bad.

A few years back I was the recipient of a blind date set up by my son and daughter-in-law. This prospect was promising. He was a medical doctor who was currently a teaching physician at a prestigious medical facility in Houston. This was going to be a highly anticipated evening and certainly one that solicited the purchase of a new ensemble. Arrangements to meet at an upper scale restaurant were now in progress.

After careful preparations and a few phone calls to establish time and location for the blind date, the evening arrived. Awkward moments are always a part of the unknown. This evening brought an entirely new meaning to the word awkward. The bar within the restaurant was the rendezvous point. His description of himself was perfect, so he was relatively easy to locate. Although he had the distinction, manner and dress of a professional, he certainly was in no shape to administer any type of medical care. And by that, I mean, he was shit-faced drunk. Using alcohol to ease awkward moments is not unusual, so I was not all that alarmed. After all, blind dates are usually awkward in the opening moments. In these situations, liquor can facilitate a calm, appearance. He had an heir of distinction. I hate to say it but I was interested.

After being seated at a very nice table with elegant ambiance and candlelight, conversation between the two of us started flowing more freely. And of course, vodka helped. Light and friendly questions about job and family were exchanged. There was significant evidence of a man that was highly intelligent, sophisticated. These are all the qualities to check mark on a "good date list."

Polite conversation continued as we surveyed the menu for dinner choices. The doctor date continued to order cocktails at a rapid pace. Either he was extremely nervous, extremely thirsty, or extremely dependent. His ability to function had started to slip. I was getting annoyed and concerned for my safety.

Nevertheless, we ordered appetizers, salad, and entrees. Our waiter was efficient and well-trained, as you would expect when it comes to fine dining. He took our order in a prompt and appropriate manner. The dynamics of the evening shifted slightly when my doctor date chastised our waiter for not taking our order. Confused, yet courteous, the young man took our order for the second time. The waiter and I exchanged confused glances but no foul, no harm. We went along with it. The slurred speech was taking its toll on the wild, romantic dreams anticipated for future dates.

Dinner arrived. Our conversation had progressed. We covered abbreviated backgrounds, anecdotal events, and life in general. The topics were light and friendly, and my date had relaxed significantly. Alcohol is funny like that. Past relationships were mentioned and habits and beliefs about life were relayed in casual tidbits.

But the quote of the evening that occurred toward the end of dinner was one that would be recorded in my slightly overstuffed memory drive forever. He looked at me with bleary eyes and said, quite calmly, "You know, honey, all men really want from a woman is to be fed and fucked."

What?!

Slightly stunned I thought that I may have misunderstood what he said. I responded with, "What did you say?"

He repeated it. I had not misunderstood. He was serious. Call me old-fashioned or naïve, but that was a moment that defined any thoughts of a future date. My goal, at that point, was to finish the evening and hope for better experiences to come.

It was certain that he would not be in my future. Most women fantasize that men desire intimacy but, certainly timing is everything and as a woman, I want those words to be chosen carefully and in the proper setting.

The evening ended unceremoniously. We both exchanged closing salutations and drove off to our separated destinations. He did call a few times, but I never returned the calls. There were debates between my children and friends as to whether the doctor deserved a second chance. Was he just inebriated and lost his inhibitions or was that him as the real deal? I will never know the answer.

Since I was the beneficiary of too many foolish relationships in my life, this time my baggage got the best of me. I decided to let feminine intuition become the loudest voice in my head.

"Happy endings are best achieved by keeping the right doors locked." Margaret Atwood, *The Penelopiad*

Three Strikes, You're Out

There is a local restaurant in my neighborhood that has become a well-known Thursday night hang out for the older crowd. It was a place where you could almost guarantee finding a man who would at least ask you to dance. My girlfriends had been bugging me for months to go, so we set off one Thursday evening to explore this new geriatric nightlife scene.

I'd been there many times for dinner but never on a Thursday night so, when we walked in the door it was exciting to see so many people our age laughing, drinking, dancing, talking and just having a great time. We settled ourselves into a table close to the piano, and ordered drinks.

I was newly divorced from a very bad second marriage, so I was very skeptical and simply planned to do my favorite thing which is "people watch." This seemed like the perfect place to do just that. As I glanced around the room, I noticed that most of the tables were filled with women, drinking, laughing and listening to music. Then I noticed the men, all sixty or over, standing around the bar scanning the tables. Some were talking to other men, but most of them were intent on searching out the room for someone. Every now and then one of them would break from the pack and invite someone to the small dance floor. They would escort them back to their table afterward and return to their spot at the bar.

Watching all of this made me wonder if this wasn't a place where gigolos hung out, but my friends assured me that the men here weren't male escorts. After all, they didn't think gigolos over sixty would make any money. It was simply a place where the older crowd came to enjoy some good music and dancing. However, I begged to differ on the money part after seeing so many desperate women—oh my God, was I part of *that* desperate group now? I also found it interesting that a lot of these men had their shirts unbuttoned down far enough to show off shiny gold chains nestled in graying chest hair. This was a sadly obvious clue that they were still living in the seventies. However, now the shirt stretched out right above that tell-tale sign of aging, the paunch.

As we sat watching the show being played out in front of us, one of these men with a gold chain started walking over to our table. He was tall, good looking, well dressed and confident which put everyone in a clamor, "Oh lordy girls," I said mimicking an exaggerated Southern accent, "Look out, he's a-walking this way!"

He approached me on the right, stuck out his hand and asked if I wanted to dance. At first, I said no, but after much prodding from my friends, I agreed and followed him out onto the dance floor. He took me firmly in his arms and proceeded to move me around the dance floor. It's easy to follow someone when they know what they're doing, and we danced together through four songs before he escorted me back to the table and went back to the bar. Several women in the crowd were shooting daggers my way as I sat down. He must be one of the bar's regulars, I thought.

My friends had a million questions once I got back to the table.

"What's his name?"

"Oh my God, you both looked so great dancing together!"

"What does he do?"

"Where does he live?"

"Did you give him your number?"

"Ladies, stop already. It was a few dances. His name is Bob, he lives right around here, he's in oil and gas and no, I didn't give him my number."

"Why not?" Jan asked.

"Because I don't know him!"

Dawn stated, "You know it's time to get back out there, so take a chance. He seems like a nice guy."

"They all seem like nice guys, until they aren't," Patty said emphatically.

I agreed.

Bob seemed to know everyone and asked several other women to dance before making his way back to our table and asking me to dance again. I figured what the hell, he's a good dancer, and followed him. We had great conversation and he made me laugh so, when he dropped me off at our table and asked for my number, I slipped him my business card. He said he'd call me to go out.

As he walked away, my friends were ecstatic but I was skeptical and never gave him much thought as I enjoyed my weekend and dug into the next work week.

Before I could blink, it was the following Thursday. When my phone buzzed late that afternoon, I checked the text message and it was from Bob. It simply said, "Meet me at the bar tonight at eight."

Having already made plans, I texted him back and said, "I'm sorry but I already have plans." No response.

In my past relationships, I would have kept texting to make sure I hadn't offended him and begged for another chance but that was the old me and the twice divorced me didn't really care.

Another work week goes by and Thursday rolls around again. Bob sends a text, "Meet me at the bar tonight at eight."

Again, having not heard from him all week, I texted him back and said, "I'm so sorry but I have to work late tonight on a deadline. Maybe tomorrow night?"

No response.

And, another week goes by and I get the Thursday text, "Meet me at the bar tonight at eight."

I responded with, "Hey, again I have to apologize but I can't go tonight. If you would have given me more notice, I could have rearranged my schedule. Would you mind meeting tomorrow or Saturday night instead?"

His response, "That's three strikes. You're out."

Now I'm really confused and mad but don't want to give him the satisfaction of knowing that he has upset me, so I simply reply, "Thank you for showing me crazy before I married you."

The following Sunday I go to my local church and who walks down the aisle, and sits two rows in front of me? Bob with a woman—who was obviously his wife!

That was a massive strikeout for me. Live and learn.

No Job, No Way

nline dating, where everyone lies about their age, weight, height, interests and pretty much everything in between! So why do we do it? Maybe loneliness, perhaps the need to connect to someone, but I think the real reason is because we can be anything or anyone we want to be. At least that has been my experience with the online dating scene. Most of my dates have been with someone completely different than their profile stated. You would think I would learn, but I will forever be a romantic at heart believing that there is that one person out there,

And he's waiting for me too.

Take Ted for example, he had an amazing profile story.

I'm a man who loves to go dancing. I "clean up real good," and know how to turn on the charm. I love spending the weekend outside exploring, barbecuing with friends, and playing with my dog. My kids are all grown with kids of their own and I love spending time with all of them when I can. If you're looking for a nice guy, I'm your man!

Sounded great—at least it did for me since I put in my profile that I was looking for my last dance partner and that I loved spending time with my kids and grandkids. His profile also said he was in business for himself. I had my own business so I appreciated the connection this would give us.

He had nice photos too. Some of them were just him—tall and handsome—but most were with him and his grandkids which I adored since my own grandkids mean so much to me. So, I sent him a "wink" and he responded with a "kiss" one night while I was eating my dinner, alone, in bed watching TV with my dogs snuggled up around me.

We spent the next few days talking via the dating app when we had time. Although, now that I can reflect on things, I was always the one playing catch up with our conversations. Anyway, one evening he sent me his phone number and asked if I could send him a text instead of talking through the app. I didn't see any harm in it because no warning bells had gone off in my head yet, so I said yes.

The next few days were filled with texts back and forth and then one evening my phone rang and it was him, calling me. I got nervous, and answered the phone with a wary hello. He had this deep radio show host voice that would make any woman swoon and as soon as I heard it, I was smitten.

Our new in-person conversations fast forwarded our online dating into real dating by the end of the week and as I dressed to go meet this man, I wondered if he would be the one I'd been searching for since my divorce ten years prior.

We met at a local restaurant we both were familiar with and one where I felt safe. I arrived first and sat at the bar where I could watch the front door, just in case he didn't look like his profile photos. I was out of there if he didn't because I'd dealt with that one on more than one occasion.

In he walked, looking just like his photos. The ice in my

heart melted a little as he walked toward me, held out his hand and said, "Hi, beautiful. You look just like your photos."

"So do you, which is a surprise, I must add," I stated a little too quickly.

Thus, began our long conversation about online dating and the weird adventures we'd both been on in the past few years. We had a lot in common it seemed and were both tired of the whole exhausting process. Maybe this one will turn out better than the rest of them.

The evening progressed with drinks, quite a few on his end but I thought he was nervous, so I let it go by without much thought. We both ordered a nice dinner and even split a dessert. When the check came, the waiter put it in the middle of the table, and we continued having a great time and conversation. Thirty minutes passed and being a self-made woman who owned her own business, I reached for the check and began looking it over. He suddenly excused himself and went to the bathroom without saying anything. I didn't find it too odd that he didn't return after ten minutes. I thought perhaps, he'd gotten sick in the bathroom. After all, he'd had quite a bit to drink and the bill certainly reflected it.

We'd been at the restaurant for almost three hours and I had a busy day coming up, so I was ready to go. I went ahead and slipped my credit card into the folder and handed it to the waiter who had plenty of time to bring it back. I signed it, closed the folder and laid it back in the middle of the table.

And magically, he reappeared and said, "Ready to go?"

I said, sure and stood up, then said. "No, wait a sec, can we sit down for a minute? I'd like to say something."

He sat back down in his chair with a harrumph.

"Look, I'm confused. I don't mind splitting the check with someone I barely know. I can pay for myself, no problem. What I don't understand is you not *offering* to pay for anything, not even the tip. And you drank a lot, so the bar part of the bill was pretty high. Am I missing something here?"

He looked over at me and said, "Hey, I lost my job in Arkansas and I've been looking for one here in Texas for the past two months so I'm kind of broke. Hope you don't mind footing the bill while I'm here the next few weeks, I'll pay you back when I get some work."

"Wait, I thought your profile stated you were born and raised in Texas and in business for yourself?"

"I am, sort of. I've been living in the Ozarks and I've been a salesman for many years, so I call it 'in business for myself.'"

"You do, do you? And you expect me to, as you put it 'foot the bill' while you're here looking for a job. Is that correct?"

"Well, when you put it that way, it sounds bad."

I stood up, grabbed my purse and walked out the door, never looking back to see if he was following or if he was already sizing up another gullible woman at the bar.

A few months later I looked him up on Facebook and let's just say that I know I dodged a bullet because he looked like a very old Leonardo di Caprio (and not in a good way) in the movie *The Revenant*, full shaggy beard and hair, and totally unkempt, back home living in a shack in the Ozarks.

Done and done.

About the Authors

Younger and (Somewhat) Naïve

Kristen Houghton is the author of the best-selling series, *A Cate Harlow Private Investigation*. Her book *Lilith Angel* is a recent Bram Stoker Award finalist.

Her non-fiction book, *And Then I'll Be Happy! Stop Sabotaging Your Happiness and Put Your Own Life First* has been called, "Life changing. An absolute must read for all women." Maria Rago, Ph.D., noted psychologist for women's issues

Houghton is also the author of nine novels, two non-fiction books, a collection of short stories, a book of essays, and a children's novella.

She has covered politics, news, and lifestyle issues as a contributor to the Huffington Post. Her writing portfolio includes Criminal Element Magazine, a division of Macmillan Publishing, Sisters-in-Crime, Today, senior fiction editor at Bella Magazine, interviews and reviews for HBO documentaries, OWN, The Oprah Winfrey Network, and The Style Channel.

Before becoming a full-time author, Kristen, who holds an Ed.D. in linguistics, taught World Languages on the high school and university levels. Along with her husband, educator and baseball historian Alan William Hopper, she is a philanthropist supporting the non-profits Project Literacy which is dedicated to teaching reading and writing skills to adults, and Shelters With Heart, which are safe havens established to house victims of domestic abuse and their pets.

The couple has three cats and a dog. All of the fur-babies are rescues. Kristen and her husband divide their time between a home on Sanibel Island and the New York City area.

Older and (Somewhat) Wiser

Sandra Morgan lives in Houston, Texas with her three doxies. In 2008, she established the magazine *Kalon Women,* where she is the Editor in Chief. The magazine is an online community with articles written specifically for the lifestyles of women over the age of fifty.

Sandra is also the CEO of a digital marketing company called The Network Chefs. She collected the stories featured in Part Two Older and (Somewhat) Wiser from her personal friends' dating experiences.

Her first book, *Learning to Hop,* is slated to be published by Skylight-NYC Publishers in 2021.

Made in the USA
Monee, IL
16 October 2020

45254867R20042